Stories From The Bible

STORIES FROM
The Bible

RETOLD BY MARY AULD

ILLUSTRATED BY DIANA MAYO

W
FRANKLIN WATTS
LONDON • SYDNEY

To my mother and my grandmother - M.A.
To Mum and Dad - D.M.

This edition first published in 2000 by
Franklin Watts, 96 Leonard Street,
London EC2A 4XD

Franklin Watts Australia
14 Mars Road, Lane Cover, NSW 2066

Series editor: Rachel Cooke
Designer: Matthew Lilly
Consultants: Reverend Richard Adfield; Laurie Rosenberg, Marlena Schmool and Samantha Blendis, the Board of Deputies of British Jews

A CIP catalogue record for this book is available from the British Library.

ISBN 0 7496 3924 5

Dewey Classification 221

Printed in Hong Kong/China

Contents

Noah's Ark

Long, long ago, God looked down at the earth and the people He had given it to. He saw that the people had filled His creation with wickedness and evil, and His heart was filled with pain. He was sorry that He had ever made men and women.

But there was one man whom God still loved. His name was Noah. Noah was a good and honest man. He lived his life with God at his side. And he had three sons: Shem, Ham and Japheth.

Now God spoke to Noah: "I have decided to

destroy all people because they have filled the earth with violence and crime. You must make yourself an ark of cypress wood, three decks deep, with many rooms. Coat it inside and out with pitch. The ark should be 300 cubits long, 50 cubits wide and 30 cubits high. There should be a window in its roof and a door on its side.

"I am going to bring a great flood and end all life on earth. Every living creature that breathes will die. But I shall make a promise - my covenant - to you: that you, your wife, your sons and their wives shall go into the ark with many animals. Inside, all shall stay safe from the Flood."

And Noah did just what God had told him to do.

Once Noah had built the ark, God spoke to him again. "You and your family must go into the ark. And you must collect together seven pairs of the animals I allow you to eat, seven males and their mates. And of every other kind of animal, you must take two, one male and one female. Of the birds that fly in the air, you must also take seven pairs, male and female. In this way, after the Flood, every kind of animal will once again be able to breed and spread across the earth. You must act now, for the rain will begin in seven days."

And Noah did everything that God told him.

Noah was six hundred years old when the Flood came. And on the day the rain started, Noah and his sons, Shem, Ham and Japheth, together with their four wives, entered the ark. And behind them came every creature that has the breath of life.

Wild animals and farm animals, the birds of the air and the creatures that creep and crawl on the earth, all went into the ark, two by two, male and female, just as God had commanded. And when they were all safely inside, God shut them in.

Now the springs of the deep burst apart and the floodgates of heaven opened. For forty days and forty nights it rained. The floodwaters rose and lifted the ark high above the earth, and it drifted out over the water.

The floodwaters continued to swell and grew still higher, until even the tops of the mountains were deep under the water. And every living thing on earth died - all the birds of the air, all the animals

that walked or wriggled upon the ground, and every single person. All life on earth was wiped out. Only Noah was left, and the others with him in the ark.

After forty days the rain stopped, but the floodwaters remained. Then God remembered Noah and the ark and sent a wind to dry up the water. The floodgates of heaven and the springs of the deep were closed. Slowly, the level of the water began to drop. Finally, the ark came to rest on the top of the mountains of Ararat.

After another forty days, Noah opened the window in the ark's roof and let out a raven, which flew to and fro until the waters on the earth had dried up.

Then Noah sent out a dove to see if the ground was dry enough to walk on. But the dove could find no dry place to rest its foot, and returned to the ark. So Noah put out his hand and took the dove back into the ark.

Finally, the ark came to rest on the top of the mountains of Ararat.

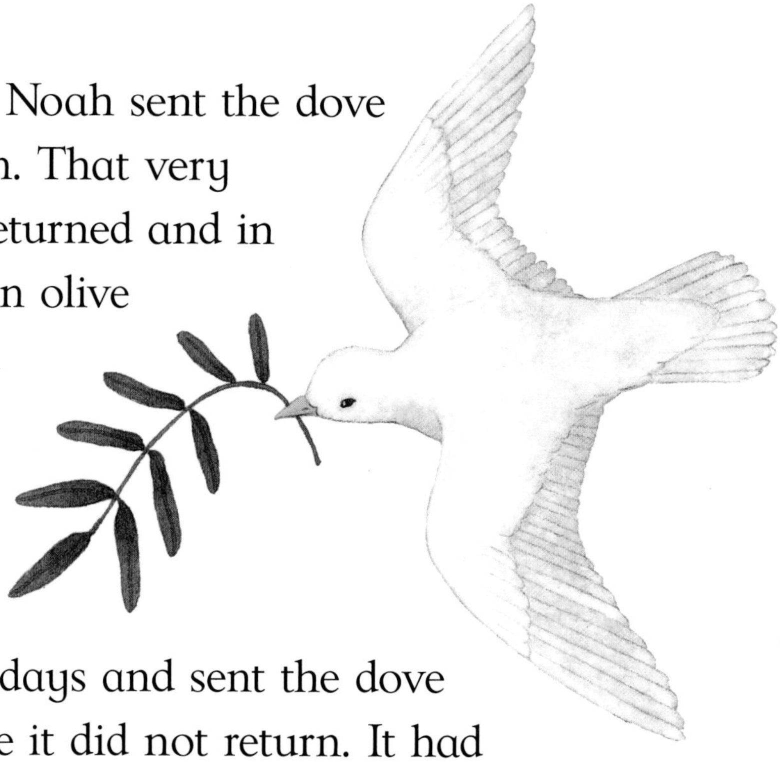

Seven days later, Noah sent the dove out of the ark again. That very evening, the dove returned and in its beak it carried an olive leaf, freshly plucked from the tree! Now Noah knew that the waters were nearly gone. He waited seven more days and sent the dove out again. This time it did not return. It had made its home elsewhere.

Noah looked out of the ark and saw that the water had all but disappeared. Soon the earth was completely dry.

God spoke to Noah. "Come out of the ark," he said, "together with your wife, your sons and their wives. Bring out all the living creatures that are with you, the birds and the beasts. Let them spread out over the earth, and be fruitful and grow in number on every part of it."

So Noah came out, together with his wife, his sons and their wives. Every animal and every bird came out with him, too, one kind after another.

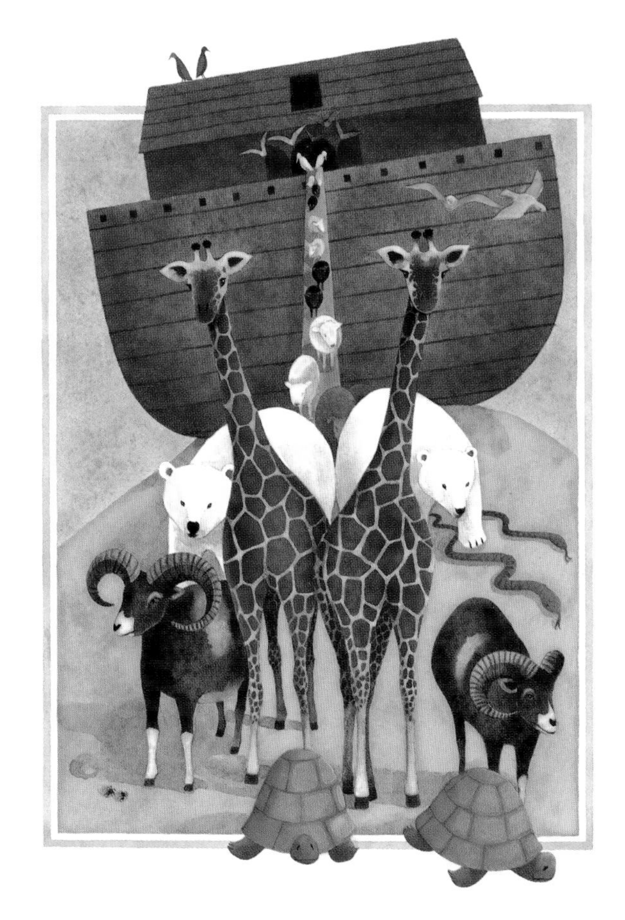

Noah built an altar to God on the mountainside, and he sacrificed burnt offerings on it. God smelt the sweet scent of the sacrifice and was pleased. He said to Himself, "I shall never again destroy the earth or the creatures that live upon it. For as long as the earth lasts, sowing and harvest, cold and heat, summer and winter, day and night will never cease."

Then God blessed Noah and his family. "Be fruitful and increase, and let your families fill the earth. All living creatures, all the beasts of the earth, the birds of the sky and the fish of the sea shall be under your control and care. I give them to you as your food just as I gave you green plants. But I shall expect something in return for this, and also for every human life. Remember, I have made humans in my image and whoever sheds the blood of

"I have set my rainbow in the clouds."

another person shall give up their life as well. Now go out into the world, let your families multiply and fill the land with people once more."

Then God said, "I give you now a new covenant, which will stand for you and all your families to come, and every living thing on earth. This is my promise: never again shall I destroy all life with a flood.

"And as a sign of this covenant between me and you and all ages to come, I have set my rainbow in the clouds. Whenever clouds gather over the earth and the rainbow appears in the sky, I will remember my covenant and the waters shall not flood again."

So Noah, his family and all the animals and birds came down from the mountains and spread out through the land. And soon their children and their children's children filled the earth with life once more.

Jacob and Esau

Long ago in the land of Canaan, Isaac, son of Abraham, married Rebekah. Isaac loved his wife but they were both sad because they had no children. Isaac prayed to God to give Rebekah a child.

God answered Isaac's prayer and Rebekah became pregnant. But there seemed to be a constant struggle inside her womb. Rebekah asked God what was happening to her.

"There are two nations in your womb," replied God. "Two separate peoples shall come out of your body. One people shall be stronger than the other; and the older will serve the younger."

And when the time came for Rebekah to give birth, she had twins.

The first twin to come out was red, and covered in hair, so they named him Esau. The second followed swiftly after, grasping his brother by the heel. Rebekah and Isaac called him Jacob.

The boys grew up. Esau became a skilful hunter, an outdoors man. Jacob was quiet and stayed at home, keeping close to the tents. Isaac

loved Esau, because he liked to eat the animals Esau caught while hunting, but Rebekah loved Jacob.

One day, Jacob was cooking a stew when Esau returned from hunting, ravenously hungry. "Give me some of that red stuff," Esau begged Jacob. "I'm famished!"

"Only if you sell me your birthright," replied Jacob, "so that I will have the right of the first-born son, not you."

"I'm about to starve to death," said Esau. "What good is a birthright to me?"

"Swear to it first," said Jacob.

So Esau swore an oath, selling his birthright to Jacob, and ate his fill of the red stew. He gave up his birthright without a second thought.

Time passed. Isaac grew old and his eyesight dimmed so that he could no longer see. He called Esau to him. "My son," he said, "I am now an old man and may soon die. Take your bow and arrow and go out and hunt some animals for me. Use them to make me one of those tasty meals that I love so much. Then I can give you my blessing before I die." So Esau set out on his hunt.

Rebekah had been listening when Isaac spoke to Esau. She found Jacob, her favourite son, and told him all she had heard. Then she said: "Listen carefully, and do just what I tell you. Go out to the flock and bring me two choice kids,

and I will make a meal for your father, just the way he likes it. Then you can take it to him and receive his blessing instead of Esau."

"But Esau is hairy, and my skin is smooth," worried Jacob. "What if my father touches me? He will think I am tricking him and curse me rather than bless me."

"The curse will be on me!" his mother replied. "Just do what I say and fetch those goats."

Jacob did as his mother told him. He brought her the kids and she prepared his father's favourite dish. Then Rebekah took Esau's best clothes and made Jacob dress in them. She also covered Jacob's hands and neck with the hairy skin of the kids. Finally, she placed the dish of food in Jacob's hands and sent him off to his father.

Isaac heard Jacob arriving. "Who is it?" he asked.

"It is Esau, your first-born," lied Jacob. "I have done as you told me. Please sit up and eat this meat so that I can receive your blessing."

"How did you find the meat so quickly?" asked Isaac.

"God gave me success," explained Jacob.

Isaac asked his son to come closer and touched his skin. "Your voice is Jacob's voice, but your hands are Esau's," he said. "Are you really my son Esau?"

"I am," said Jacob.

So Isaac ate the meal and then kissed his son. As he did so, he smelt Esau's clothes on Jacob. "Ah, the smell of my

son is like the smell of the fields that God has blessed," Isaac exclaimed and he blessed Jacob, saying, "May God give you riches from heaven and earth. Let peoples serve you and nations bow down to you. Be lord over your brothers. Cursed are those that curse you and blessed are those who bless you."

No sooner had Isaac finished his blessing and Jacob left than Esau returned from hunting. He prepared the meal and went to Isaac. "Please sit up, my father," he said, "and eat this meat so that I can receive your blessing."

"Who are you?" demanded Isaac.

"I am Esau, your first-born son," replied Esau.

Isaac began to tremble violently. "Who was it who brought me a meal just now?" he asked. "I blessed him - and he will remain blessed! Your brother has taken your blessing."

"Jacob has already taken my birthright and now he has my blessing. Have you no blessing for me?" Esau asked Isaac.

"I have made Jacob lord over you and given him riches," his father replied. "What can I possibly give you?"

"Have you only one blessing? Bless me, too, Father!" begged Esau. And he broke into loud sobs.

So Isaac blessed Esau. "You will live by the sword and you will serve your brother. But when you grow restless, you will break his yoke from your neck."

Now Esau held a grudge against Jacob. "After my father dies, I shall kill Jacob," he said to himself. But Rebekah heard of his plans. She went to Jacob and told him to run away. "Go to my brother Laban," she urged him. "Stay with him until Esau is no longer angry and has forgotten what you've done."

Afterwards, Rebekah spoke to Isaac and persuaded him to let Jacob go to Laban, who lived far away in the city of Haran. Isaac agreed and called Jacob to him and told him to leave.

"Marry one of Laban's daughters," Isaac commanded. Then he added, "May God Almighty bless you and make your family grow so that you become a great people. May He give you and your children the blessing He gave Abraham so that you will have this land, the land He gave to Abraham."

And Jacob set out for his uncle's home.

Before the sun had set, Jacob stopped for the night. With a stone for his pillow he lay down and slept. And he dreamed of a stairway that stretched from the earth to heaven with the angels of God walking up and down it. God stood above the stairway and spoke to Jacob: "I am the Lord, the God of Abraham and Isaac. I give the land on which you lie to you and your children. Your family will be like the dust of the earth and spread out in all directions and bring blessing to all its people. Remember, I am with you and will protect you wherever you go. I shall bring you back to this land."

Jacob awoke amazed. Using his stone pillow, he built a pillar and poured oil on it, and continued on his way. Later, he called the place Bethel, the house of God.

Jacob lived with his uncle Laban for twenty years. He did well. He married both of Laban's daughters, Leah and Rachel, and, with them and their two maids, he had twelve sons and a daughter. But one day God told him it was time to go back to Canaan.

With all his new family, his servants and flocks of goats, sheep, donkeys and camels, Jacob set out for home.

Jacob was frightened of meeting Esau. He realised now the wrong he had done him, and he sent his servants ahead with gifts of many animals. But he need not have worried: Esau greeted his brother with joy, embracing him and weeping. Jacob wept, too. Both brothers knew that God had chosen Jacob and his children to have the land of Canaan. Jacob had come home.

Joseph and His Brothers

There once was a man called Jacob who lived in the land of Canaan. Jacob had twelve sons and one daughter. His sons looked after his flocks of sheep in the hills and valleys around his home.

Of all his sons, Jacob loved his eleventh son, Joseph, the best, because he had been born when Jacob was growing old. Joseph worked alongside his brothers and told Jacob what they did wrong. And Jacob gave his favourite son a beautiful coat, decorated with many different colours.

Joseph's brothers were jealous. They hated Joseph and were unkind to him. They became even angrier when Joseph told them of his amazing dreams. In one, his brothers' sheaves of corn bowed down to Joseph's; and in another dream, the sun, the moon and eleven stars bowed down to Joseph as well. Did the dreams mean that Joseph would one day be more important than the rest of his family? Would they have to bow to him like a king? His brothers didn't like Joseph's dreams, and they hated him all the more.

One day, Joseph set out to join his brothers, who were with their flocks far from home. The brothers saw Joseph coming: "Look, it's the dreamer. Let's kill him and see what comes of his dreams!" So they grabbed Joseph, ripped off his coat and threw him into a dry pit to die.

Soon after some merchants passed by, their camels laden with spices to be sold in Egypt. "Let's sell Joseph rather than kill him," suggested one plotter. "He is our brother after all!" So they sold Joseph as a slave to the merchants, for twenty pieces of silver.

The brothers tore up Joseph's coat and covered it with goat's blood, and took it to their father. Jacob was heartbroken: Joseph had clearly been torn to pieces by a wild animal. Nothing his family said could comfort him.

When the merchants arrived in Egypt, they sold Joseph to an Egyptian called Potiphar, a rich and important officer in the court of Pharaoh, king of Egypt. He liked Joseph, who worked hard for him, and soon put him in charge of his whole household. God was looking after Joseph.

All was going well until Potiphar's wife became interested in Joseph. He was very handsome and she wanted him to be her lover. Again and again she asked him but Joseph always refused. How could he betray his master? How could he sin against God?

Potiphar's wife grew angry. She went to her husband and told him Joseph had tried to kiss her and more. Potiphar was furious. He had Joseph thrown instantly into prison.

Even in prison, God watched over Joseph, for it was there he met two of Pharaoh's servants, his butler and his baker, who had got into trouble with their master.

One morning, Joseph found the two men in great distress. They had both had strange dreams

in the night and were sure they must mean something. First the butler told his story. "I dreamt that I stood in front of a vine laden with ripe grapes. And I took the grapes and pressed them in Pharaoh's wine cup and gave the cup to him, and he drank all the wine."

With the help of God, Joseph explained the butler's dream. "Pharaoh will soon forgive you. You will be freed and once again give Pharaoh his cup."

Now the baker told his dream. "I dreamt that I had baskets of bread on my head to take to Pharaoh, but before I could give them to him, some birds ate all the bread."

This dream was not so good. "Pharaoh will have your head chopped off," Joseph told the unhappy baker. And within three days, both dreams had come true. The butler was once again at Pharaoh's side and the baker was dead.

Back at his work, the butler forgot all about Joseph, even though Joseph had begged him for help. But then something happened to remind him: Pharaoh had been dreaming, two extraordinary dreams, and no one, not even his wisest magician, could tell him what they meant. Joseph was summoned to the court.

His hair cut and with new clothes, Joseph stood before Pharaoh. "It is not I, but God who will tell you the meaning of your dreams," he said.

So Pharaoh began: "I dreamt I was standing by the Nile, when seven strong, well-fed cows came out of the river and began to feed. Then seven more cows appeared, but they were thin and scrawny - uglier than I have ever seen. And these skinny cows ate up the fat ones, but they stayed as thin as before.

"Then I dreamt a second dream. This time seven ears of good, ripe corn grew up, but then seven more ears grew, shrivelled and windswept, and they swallowed up the good corn. Can you tell me what no other man has known?"

"Your dreams mean the same thing," said Joseph. "The

seven fat cows and the healthy ears of corn are seven years of plenty when Egypt will have good harvests. The seven skinny cows and the shrivelled ears are seven years of terrible famine, which will follow.

"This is caused by God," explained Joseph. "You must appoint a wise man to prepare for the famine by organising food to be stored during the seven years of good harvest."

Pharaoh was impressed. "With the knowledge God has given you, there is surely none so wise as you," he said to Joseph. "You are the man to prepare Egypt for the famine. Only I shall be more powerful than you." And he gave Joseph his ring and fine linen to wear, and put a gold chain around his neck.

And, as Joseph had predicted, there were seven years of good harvests and then came awful famine, which spread throughout the world. Only in Egypt was there enough food for everyone because Joseph had made sure that there was plenty of grain in store.

Pharoah gave Joseph his ring and fine linen to wear, and put a gold chain around his neck.

In Canaan, Joseph's family was starving. "You must go to Egypt and buy some grain," Jacob told his remaining sons. So Joseph's brothers set out for Egypt. Only Benjamin, Joseph's youngest brother, stayed behind.

Joseph controlled the sale of grain in Egypt, so it was to him the brothers went. They bowed low before the Pharaoh's magnificent officer - they did not realise it was Joseph at all. But Joseph recognised them, and he remembered his dreams.

Joseph decided to test his brothers. He gave them grain but made them promise to return to Egypt with Benjamin to prove they were trustworthy. He would keep one brother captive until they returned.

At first, Jacob would not let Benjamin go. He was terrified that he would lose him as he had lost Joseph. But eventually the famine forced him to allow his sons to return to Egypt.

This time Joseph gave his brothers a splendid welcome. There was a great feast and the brothers' sacks were filled with grain. Secretly, Joseph told his servants to hide a silver cup in Benjamin's sack. Then he sent his brothers on their way. Still none of them had recognised him.

The brothers had not gone far when Joseph sent his servants after them. They searched the sacks and found Joseph's precious cup in Benjamin's grain. "Our master will make you his slave for this theft," warned one servant and they took the brothers back to Joseph's house.

The brothers begged Joseph for mercy. "Our father has already lost one son. Without Benjamin, he will surely die. Take me as your slave instead!" offered one brother.

Joseph could no longer hold back. In tears, he told his

brothers who he was. They were speechless. What would Joseph do to them?

"Don't worry," he said. "God has wished it this way. If I hadn't come to Egypt, we would all have died in the famine. Now I can provide for us all - you must bring all our family to Egypt."

So Jacob and his family came to Egypt, as God had planned. Joseph met his father and embraced him. Father and son stayed in each other's arms for a long time. Egypt was now home to them both.

Moses in the Bulrushes

There once was a Hebrew called Jacob, whom God had named Israel. He and his family had come to Egypt to live with his son Joseph, who was chief adviser to Pharaoh, king of Egypt. After Jacob and his sons died, their families continued to grow and the Children of Israel spread throughout the land of Egypt.

Now a new Pharaoh became king. He was worried by the Israelites. "We must control their numbers or they may join our enemies and fight us in war," he warned. So the Egyptians made the Israelites their slaves and forced them to work for them. Yet their numbers continued to grow.

The Egyptians began to fear the Israelites. They treated them cruelly and worked them still harder. Pharaoh even ordered the midwives, who helped at the birth of Hebrew children, to kill any baby boys that were born. But the midwives feared God and did not do as Pharaoh asked. The number of Israelites still continued to grow.

Now Pharaoh made a terrible decision. He ordered his people to throw every boy baby born to the Israelites into the River Nile.

At this time, a certain man and woman among the Israelites married, and, in due course, had a baby son. The woman looked at her baby - he was beautiful. How could she kill him? For three months, she hid him at home.

After Jacob and his sons died, their families continued to grow and the Children of Israel spread throughout the land of Egypt.

When she could no longer keep the boy safely hidden, she found a wicker basket and sealed it with tar and pitch. She put her son in the basket and left it among the bulrushes at the edge of the Nile. Some way off, his sister watched to see what would happen.

Pharaoh's daughter came down to the Nile to bathe that day, while her attendants walked along the bank. So it was she who first spotted the basket amongst the reeds and ordered her slave girl to fetch it. Pharaoh's daughter opened up the basket and found the baby crying inside. She felt great pity for the boy, "This must be a Hebrew child," she said.

Now the boy's sister came forward: "Shall I

fetch a Hebrew nurse to look after the baby?" she offered, and when Pharaoh's daughter agreed, she rushed straight to her mother and brought her to the riverside.

"Take this child and nurse it for me," said Pharaoh's daughter. "I shall pay you a good wage."

And the woman took back her baby and nursed him at her home.

When the boy was old enough, his mother took him to the palace. Pharaoh's daughter adopted the child and made him her son. "I shall call him Moses," she said, which means "drawn from the water".

Moses grew to be a man in the court of the Egyptians, but he did not forget his true family. One day, as he watched a group of Hebrews labouring, he saw an Egyptian beating one of them. Thinking no one was watching, Moses killed the Egyptian and buried his body in the sand.

The next day, he saw two Hebrews fighting each other. He tried to stop them but they just said, "Who are you to tell us to stop fighting? Will you kill us like you killed the Egyptian?"

Moses was frightened. People knew about the murder and, as soon as Pharaoh heard of it, he would want Moses dead, too. So Moses ran away, leaving Egypt for the land of Midian.

Moses was sitting exhausted by a well when the seven daughters of the priest of Midian came to draw water for their sheep and goats. Some shepherds drove the girls away, but Moses took their side, and then helped them to give water to their flock.

To thank Moses, the girls' father, Jethro, invited him to

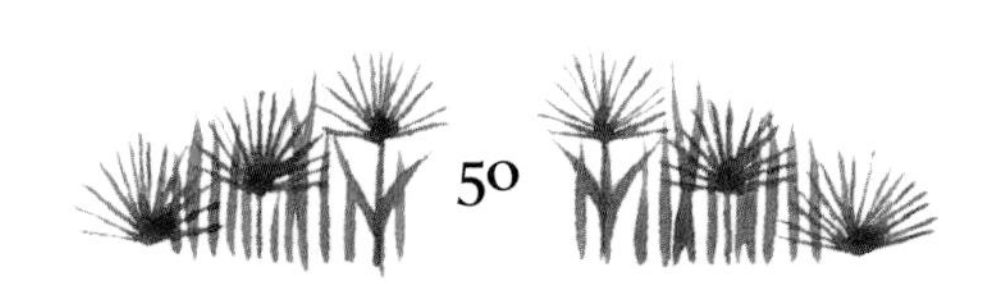

stay. Moses was happy to find a home. Even better, the priest gave Moses his daughter Zipporah as a wife. Soon they had a son called Gershom, which meant stranger. "For I have been a stranger in a foreign land," said Moses.

While Moses tended his father-in-law's flock in Midian, the Israelites in Egypt continued to suffer. There was a new king, but he was just as harsh as the old one. The Children of Israel were groaning under the weight of their slavery and they cried to God for help. And God heard them.

One day, Moses drove his sheep into the wilderness and on to the slopes of Horeb, the mountain of God. There he saw a strange sight: a bush on fire, but although the flames burned brightly, the bush was not burnt up by them. Moses turned to have a better look.

As he did so, a voice called out to him from the bush, "Moses! Moses!"

"Here I am," replied Moses.

"Do not come any closer, but take off your sandals, for you are standing on holy ground," commanded the voice. "I am God, the God of your fathers, the God of Abraham, Isaac and Jacob."

Moses was afraid and hid his face - he did not want to look upon God.

"I have come to take my people, the Children of Israel, away from slavery," God continued. "I shall take them out of Egypt to a new land - a land flowing with milk and honey. You must go to Pharaoh for me now so that you can lead my people out of Egypt."

Moses was amazed. "Who am I that you should ask me to do such a thing?"

"I shall be with you," replied God. "You will speak in my name."

"When I go to my people, what name should I give you?" asked Moses.

"I am who I am," replied God. "Tell them 'I am' has sent you to them."

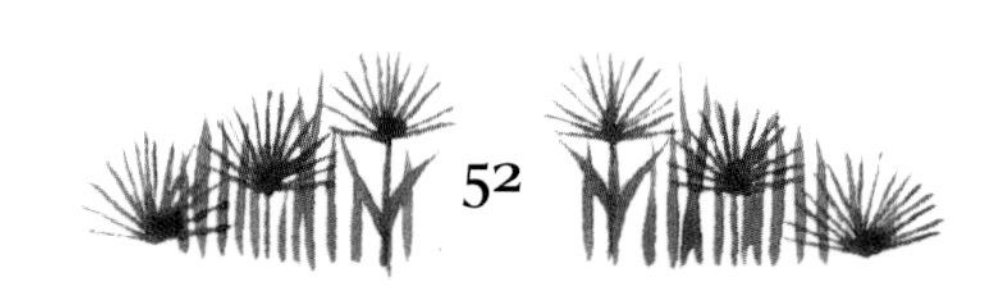

And God explained to Moses what he should do; how he must tell the Israelites of God's promise and how he should ask Pharaoh to let the Israelites travel into the desert to worship God.

And God gave Moses three signs to show his power. First, he told Moses to throw his wooden staff on the ground. Instantly, it became a snake but when Moses picked it up by its tail, the snake became a staff once more.

Second, God told Moses to put his hand inside his cloak and draw it out again. When he did this, Moses found his hand had become diseased and covered in white scales, like snow. He put his hand back inside his cloak and drew it out again. His hand was healthy once more.

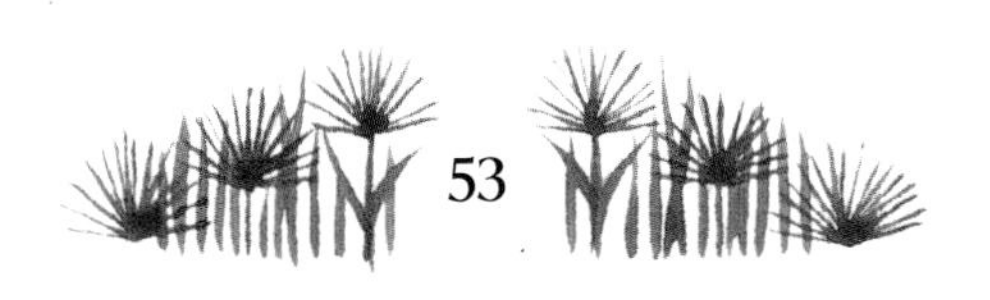

"If they don't believe either of these signs," said God, "then here is a third: take water from the Nile and pour it on the ground. It will turn into blood."

Moses was still worried: "Even with these signs, I am not good at speaking and arguing with people."

"Didn't I give you your mouth and tongue? I will help you speak and teach you what to say," said God.

But Moses said, "Lord, please ask someone else to do it."

God became angry. "Your brother Aaron will speak for you. He is on his way to meet you. You will be to him as I am to you - you will tell him what to say. And you will carry the staff so you can perform the signs."

Moses returned to his wife and her family. "Let me go back to my own people in Egypt to see how they are," he asked his father-in-law, Jethro.

"Go in peace," Jethro replied.

So Moses set out for Egypt once more with his family. In his hand he carried God's staff. He realised now why he had been saved from the bulrushes all those years ago. He was the one whom God had chosen to free the Israelites from slavery. One day, he hoped, he would bring them to the land flowing with milk and honey, the good land that God had promised.

Moses set out for Egypt once more with his family.

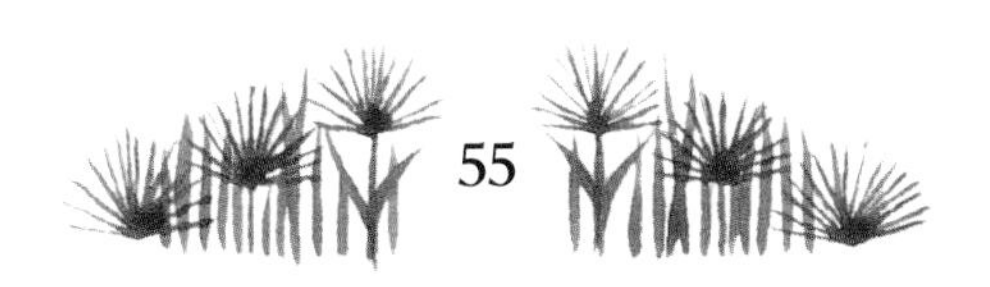

Exodus from Egypt

Long ago, God's chosen people, the Israelites, were slaves in Egypt. The Egyptians worked them hard and treated them badly, and the Israelites cried out to God for help.

God heard their cries. He decided He would free the Israelites from Egypt and take them to their own land. He chose a man called Moses to lead them. Moses would have to persuade Pharaoh, the king of Egypt, to let the Israelites go. But Moses was a poor speaker, so his brother Aaron was asked to talk for him. Moses would tell Aaron what to say, just as God told Moses.

Moses and Aaron went to Pharaoh and said: “The Lord, the God of Israel, says to you: ‘Let my people go, so that they may worship me in the desert’.”

But Pharaoh replied, “Who is the Lord? I don’t know him, and I will not let the Israelites go.”

That same day Pharaoh gave orders to his slave-drivers to work the Israelites still harder. They already made bricks, but now they had to gather the straw to mix into the brick mud as well. And they had to produce as many bricks as before.

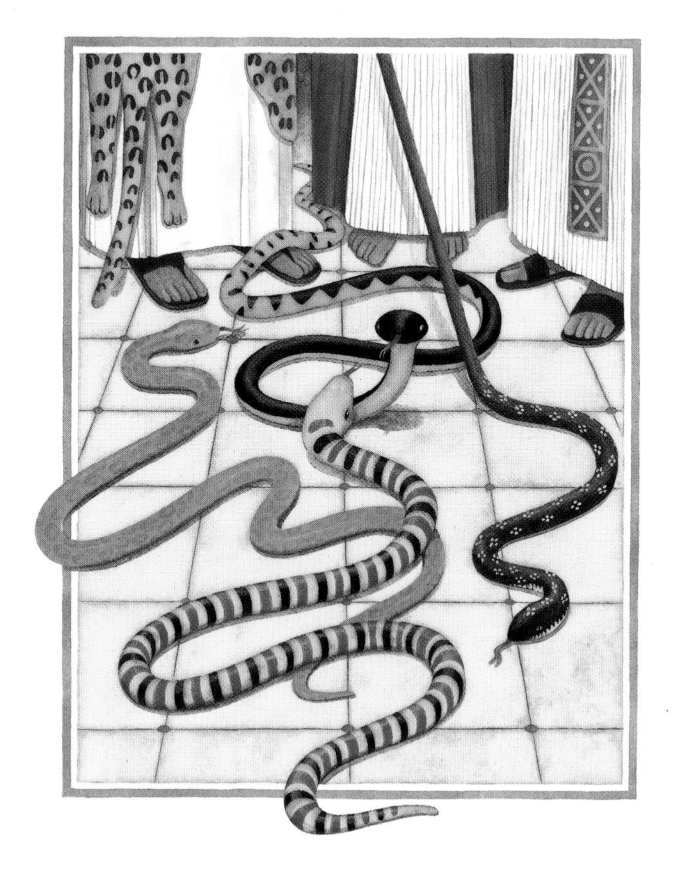

When the Israelites complained to Pharaoh, he was furious. "Lazy, that's what you are - lazy!" he cried. "All you want to do is go into the desert and make sacrifices to your Lord. Now get back to work."

Moses was unhappy. He spoke to God. "Why have you brought trouble on my people? Is this why you sent me?"

God replied: "Go with Aaron again to Pharaoh. Ask again to bring the children of Israel out of Egypt. Pharaoh will not listen. I shall harden his heart but then I shall show him my power with signs and marvels. The Egyptians will know that I am the Lord."

So Moses and Aaron went again to Pharaoh. This time, to show God's power, Moses told Aaron to throw his staff on the floor. Instantly, it became a snake.

Pharaoh summoned his magicians. Each of them threw down his staff and each staff became a snake. So, even though Aaron's snake swallowed the others, Pharaoh would not listen to Moses, just as God had said.

Now God sent ten great plagues. First, He told Moses to go to Pharaoh again. "Meet the king by the edge of the Nile. Aaron must stretch his staff out across the river. Its waters will turn to blood - there shall be blood throughout the land."

Moses and Aaron did as God commanded. As Pharaoh and his courtiers watched, Aaron struck the Nile with his staff and its water turned to blood. All the fish in the river died and the water smelled so bad that the Egyptians could not drink it.

But again Pharaoh's magicians could perform similar tricks. Pharaoh returned to his palace and refused to change his mind.

A week passed and Moses went again to Pharaoh. "The Lord says: 'Let my people go or I will plague your whole country with frogs. They will come into your palaces and your bed. They will climb all over you'."

And, when Pharaoh still refused God's demand, the frogs came and covered the land. Pharaoh's magicians called up frogs as well, but this time Pharaoh was frightened. He summoned Moses and said, "Beg your God to remove the frogs and I shall let your people go."

Moses did as Pharaoh asked. The frogs died and were piled into heaps, and the land reeked of them. But when Pharaoh saw the problem was gone, he changed his mind. The Israelites must stay in Egypt.

So God sent a new plague - a plague of lice that crawled over all the Egyptian people and their animals. Pharaoh's

magicians could not copy this marvel. "This is the finger of God," they told their king. But Pharaoh refused to listen.

And Moses said to Pharaoh, "The Lord says: 'Let my people go or I shall send a plague of insects. They will cover your houses, but the Israelites' homes will remain untouched'." The great swarms came and Pharaoh said he would let the Israelites go if Moses would remove the insects. But when they were gone, Pharaoh again went back on his word.

And so it continued - God sent plague after plague and each time Pharaoh would agree to let the Israelites go but, as soon as God removed each plague, his heart would harden and he would break his promise, just as God had said.

There was a plague which killed all the Egyptians' cattle and sheep, then another which caused boils and ulcers to break out on all the Egyptians and their animals. Pharaoh's magicians had so many boils that they could not stand before Moses.

Next came terrible storms: Moses raised his staff to the sky and God sent down hailstones mixed with thunder and lightning. The stones battered the Egyptians' barley and flax, but left the Israelites' crops untouched.

The Egyptians were becoming desperate. "Let the Israelites go," the courtiers said to Pharaoh. "Can't you see Egypt is ruined?" But when Pharaoh spoke to Moses he offered to let only the Israelite men leave Egypt, not their women and children.

In reply, Moses stretched out his staff across the land. This time God sent a swarm of locusts that ate everything

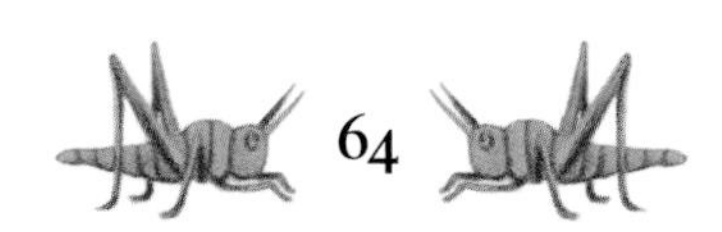

that the hail had not destroyed: the Egyptians' wheat, the fruit in their trees. Nothing green remained.

Once again, Pharaoh agreed to let the Israelites go if God would remove the locusts and, once again, when the locusts had gone, he broke his word. So God sent a great darkness over Egypt, which lasted three days. No one could see anyone else or leave his place. God gave only the Israelites light to see by.

But still Pharaoh would not agree to Moses's demands.

Now God spoke to Moses: "I shall bring one more plague on Egypt. After that Pharaoh will let you go.

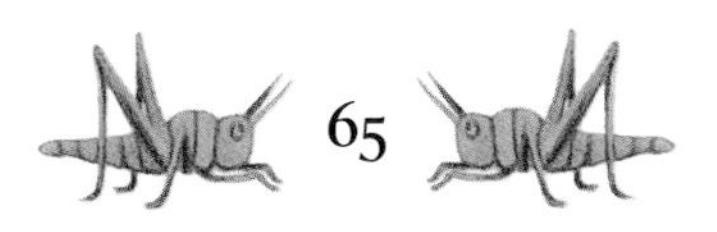

Tell the Israelites to prepare for a meal: each household shall kill a lamb. They shall put some of its blood around the doorways of their houses. Then they shall roast the lamb and eat it. That night I shall pass through Egypt and kill every firstborn son. But where I see blood on the door, I shall know to pass over that house. Death will not strike the Israelites as it does the Egyptians."

And Moses told the Israelites all that God had said and they did as He commanded. And at midnight on that day, God struck down all the firstborn sons of Egypt, from the firstborn of Pharaoh, who sat on the throne, to the firstborn of the prisoner, who was in the dungeon. A loud cry rose up from the Egyptians, for there was not one house without someone dead.

Pharaoh called Moses and Aaron in the middle of the night. "Get up and go from among my people, you and the Israelites. Go worship the Lord as you have asked!" And all the Egyptians urged the Israelites to leave.

So the Israelites took their belongings and set out from Egypt. There were about six hundred thousand men on foot, along with women and children. They took their flocks and their herds, and on their shoulders they carried dough without any yeast, because they did not have time to prepare the bread properly. And they journeyed towards the Red Sea, with God ahead to guide them, by day in a pillar of cloud and by night in a pillar of fire.

Now Pharaoh began to regret his decision. He had his chariot made ready and, with a vast army, set out in pursuit of the Israelites.

The Israelites were camping by the shores of the Red Sea when they saw the Pharaoh's armies. Terrified, they cried out to God. Moses reassured them. "God will

save you. You will never see the Egyptians again. Just stand firm." And, following God's orders, Moses raised his staff and stretched out his hand across the sea. The waters parted and the Israelites went across the sea on dry land, a wall of water on their right and a wall of water on their left.

Pharaoh, with all his soldiers, chariots and horses, followed. But God made the wheels of the chariots stick and it was difficult for them to move forward. The Egyptians began to panic.

When all the Israelites had safely crossed the sea, Moses turned and stretched out his hand across the water. The walls of water broke down and flooded together again, covering Pharaoh and his entire army. All the Egyptians drowned.

Finally, the Israelites knew they were safe. They had seen God's power and they had faith in Him and His servant Moses. Miriam, Moses's sister, took a tambourine, and with all the other women danced and sang in praise of God, who had led them out of Egypt.

David and Goliath

Long ago, the people of Israel asked the prophet Samuel to choose them a king. Samuel prayed and spoke to God and, at God's wish, he chose a man called Saul to be the Israelites' king.

Saul was a brave warrior, but he did not always listen to God or follow His commands. God became unhappy with Saul as king, and He spoke again to the prophet Samuel.

"You must visit the town of Bethlehem," He told Samuel. "Take a heifer with you as a sacrifice and go to the house of Jesse. Ask Jesse and his family to help you with the sacrifice. Then I shall point out one of his sons, whom you must anoint with oil. This son shall one day be king of Israel."

And Samuel set out for Bethlehem.

When he arrived, Samuel went straight to Jesse's house. He told Jesse and his family to prepare for the sacrifice and a feast. As the family gathered together, Samuel met Jesse's eldest son, Eliab. Surely, Samuel thought, this handsome man would be God's choice. But God said to him, "Don't judge Eliab by his appearance. He is not my choice. Remember, you can only see what a man looks like. I can see into his heart." So Samuel passed on to Jesse's next son, and the one after that, and then yet another, until he had seen seven of his sons. But still God did not show His choice.

"Haven't you any other sons?" Samuel asked Jesse.

"There is only my youngest, David, who is away looking after the sheep," replied Jesse.

So David was sent for and brought before Samuel. The boy was rosy-cheeked and bright-eyed. "This is the one," said God to Samuel. Then the prophet arose and anointed David with oil. From that day onwards, the spirit of God filled David and was always with him.

Meanwhile, King Saul was ill. God had set an evil spirit on him, which teased and terrified him.

Whenever the evil spirit came upon the king, David would pick up his harp and play.

"We must find someone who can play the harp," said Saul's courtiers. "The music will soothe the king."

Saul ordered his attendants to find a good harp-player, and one of them thought of the shepherd David. A message went to Jesse asking for his son, so Jesse sent David to the king, together with a donkey laden with gifts: bread, wine and a young goat.

Saul liked David very much. Whenever the evil spirit came upon the king, David would pick up his harp and play, and Saul would relax and the evil spirit leave him.

Sometime after, the Philistines gathered an army together to fight against Israel. Saul and the Israelites prepared for battle, too.

The Israelites pitched their camp on one hill and the Philistines on another, with the narrow valley of Elah between them.

A champion came forward from the Philistine ranks called Goliath of Gath. He was a giant of a man, standing over nine feet tall. His helmet and body armour were all made of gleaming bronze, as was the javelin slung across his back. The point of his massive spear was made of iron. His shield-bearer marched in front of him.

Goliath shouted across to the Israelite army. "Why do you need to fight a battle? Instead, choose one man to fight me - if he kills me, the Philistines will become your slaves, but if I kill him, you will become our slaves and serve us."

Goliath's challenge terrified Saul and all his people. Who could possibly take on such a man?

At this time, David had returned to his father Jesse to tend the sheep, but his three eldest brothers served in Saul's army. Jesse said to David, "Take this food to your brothers in the valley of Elah and bring me back news of them."

Early next morning, David set out as Jesse ordered, leaving someone else in charge of his sheep. He arrived at the Israelite camp just as the soldiers were taking up their battle positions, shouting a war cry. David ran to the battle lines and greeted his people.

Just as David spoke, Goliath stepped out from the Philistines'

A champion came forward from the Philistine ranks called Goliath of Gath. He was a giant of a man, standing over nine feet tall.

"I have killed both a lion and a bear to protect my father's sheep," said David.

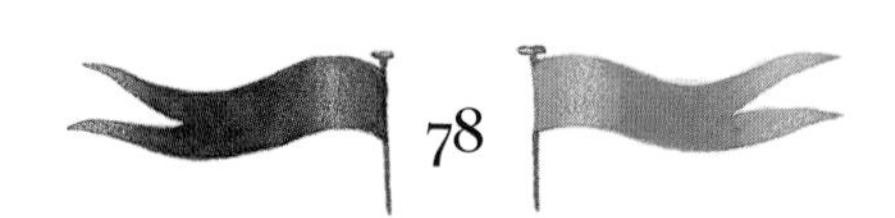

ranks and shouted his challenge once again. David heard it and saw how the Israelites fled from the giant in terror.

Word went around the Israelite camp, "The king will reward whoever kills Goliath with great wealth - and give him his daughter in marriage."

David heard the soldiers' talk and spoke to them. "Who does this Philistine think he is? How dare he defy the armies of God?" he asked.

When Eliab, David's eldest brother, heard this fighting talk, he was furious. "Why did you come here?" he demanded. "I know what a show-off you can be. You are only here to watch the battle!"

"Now what have I done?" said David. "I was only asking." And he turned away and spoke to someone else about Goliath and the reward.

Soon Saul heard about David's questions and sent for him.

David said to Saul, "Don't be frightened of Goliath. I shall fight him."

"You can't fight the Philistine," replied Saul. "You are just a boy and he has been a warrior for many years."

"I have killed both a lion and a bear to protect my father's sheep," said David. "The Philistine is just like them. God protected me from the claws of the lion and the bear, and He will keep me safe from Goliath."

"Then go," said Saul, "and may God be with you."

Then Saul dressed David in his own tunic. He put a bronze helmet on David's head and a breastplate around his body. David fastened on a sword and then tried walking around.

"I can't wear all this," he said. "I'm just not used to it." So he took off the armour. Instead, David chose five smooth stones from a nearby stream and put them in his shepherd's

bag. He took his staff in one hand and his sling in the other and went to meet Goliath.

Goliath and his shield-bearer came forward to meet David. When the Philistine saw that David was just a fresh-faced boy, he laughed nastily and cursed him. "Am I a dog that you mean to fight with a stick? Come here, I'll kill you and feed your body to the birds and animals!" jeered Goliath.

But David was not frightened. He cried out, "You may have your weapons, but I come against you in the name of God. Today, when I strike you down, the whole world will see that there is a God in Israel," and he ran towards Goliath. Reaching into his bag and taking out a stone, he slung it and struck the Philistine straight on the forehead. Goliath toppled forward on to the ground.

David stood over Goliath and cut off his head with the giant's own sword. When the Philistines saw that their champion was dead, they turned and ran. With a war cry, the men of Israel followed them and chased them right to the gates of Ekron, a great Philistine city, killing many as they went.

David took Goliath's head to Jerusalem and brought it before Saul.

"Who are you?" Saul asked him in amazement.

"I am the son of your servant Jesse of Bethlehem," said David simply. Perhaps then Saul realised he was looking in the face of the next king of Israel.

Daniel in the Lions' Den

There was once a king called Darius who ruled the mighty Persian empire from the city of Babylon. Darius had to control his huge empire - and collect his taxes - so he appointed over a hundred officers to help him. One of these officers was Daniel.

Daniel was not a Persian, he was Jewish. He had been brought to serve in the Babylonian court when his own city, Jerusalem, was captured by the Persians. Daniel was an excellent officer and a good man. Darius saw this and decided to put Daniel in charge of all his officers.

The other officers were not happy about this decision. They looked for mistakes in Daniel's work. But hard as they looked, they could find nothing wrong: Daniel was an honest man, loyal to the king and good at his job.

Then the plotters had an idea: "We will never find anything wrong with Daniel except that he is a Jew. He follows the laws of his God first, not the king's.

Let's see if we can use this against him."

So the officers went all together to the king. They bowed down low before him. "King Darius live for ever!" they cried.

"We, your loyal servants, believe that you must make a new law. You must decree that, over the next thirty days, no one should pray to any god or man other than yourself. If anyone disobeys this, they must be thrown into the den of lions.

"Proclaim this law now, oh mighty king, and write it down so that it cannot be changed. No law of Persia can be changed once it is signed by the king."

And Darius did as they asked.

Daniel heard all about the king's new law. Yet he continued to do as he had always done. Every day, three times a day, he went home and, in front of his bedroom window which faced Jerusalem, he prayed and gave thanks to God.

The men who plotted against Daniel were watching his house. They saw him praying to God and asking Him for help. And they went straight to King Darius.

"Isn't it true that you have signed a law saying that anyone who prays to any god or man except you shall be thrown to the lions?" the officers asked Darius.

"I have," replied Darius, "under the laws of Persia, which cannot change."

This was the answer the plotters wanted. "Daniel the Jew has not obeyed you, oh King," they said. "He still prays to his God three times a day."

Darius was horrified. He did not want Daniel to die. All day, he tried to find a way to save him. But as the sun set, the officers returned: "The law of Persia says that no law you have made can be changed," they reminded the king.

Darius had no choice. He gave his orders, and Daniel was arrested and thrown into the lions' den. "May the God, whom you worship so constantly, save you!" said the king to Daniel.

Darius had no choice. He gave his orders, and Daniel was arrested and thrown into the lions' den.

And a great stone was put over the mouth of the den. First Darius sealed the stone in position with his own signet ring, then his officers did the same. The king's decision was final - it could not be changed.

Darius returned to his palace. All that night, he could not sleep. All he could think about was Daniel.

He did not eat and he refused to have any music played for him.

The palace was very quiet.

The next morning, as soon as it was light, the king was up. He quickly made his way to the lions' den.

At the entrance, Darius paused. Without hope, he called

out, "Daniel, servant of the living God, has your God been able to save you from the lions?"

And to the king's amazement Daniel's voice replied: "Oh King, live for ever!"

Still sealed in his prison, Daniel described what had happened.

"My God sent an angel during the night. The angel kept the lions' mouths shut for all that time. He did this because I have done nothing wrong in the eyes of God - and, oh King, I have done nothing to hurt you."

Darius was delighted that Daniel was still alive. He ordered him to be lifted out of the den. And when this was done, everyone could see that Daniel was unharmed. His faith in God had saved him.

The officers who had plotted against Daniel were not so fortunate. For now King Darius ordered that they should be cast into the lions' den instead, along with their families.

"The angel kept the lions' mouths shut for all that time."

And before they had even reached the den's floor, the lions pounced on them and killed them.

King Darius gave out a new decree to all the people of his empire.

"Peace be with you all. I, King Darius, make a new law: in every part of my kingdom people must fear and worship the God of Daniel. He is the living God, who

shall be for ever and whose kingdom will never end. He shall rule for always.

"He rescues and saves, and He can perform great miracles, both on earth and in heaven. He has saved Daniel from the lions."

And so Daniel was once again chief officer for Darius, and he remained happy and successful for the rest of the wise king's reign.

The Story of Jonah

Long ago in the land of Canaan there lived a man called Jonah. He was a prophet and God often spoke to him.

One day God told Jonah to go to the great city of Nineveh. "The people there are full of wickedness," He said. "You must tell them to change their ways."

But Jonah ran away from God. He went to the port of Joppa and found a boat that was about to sail to a place far from Nineveh. The sailors would take him with them - for a fee. So he paid his fare and clambered on board.

The boat had not sailed far, when God sent a great wind across the sea. The wind pushed up huge waves, which

battered against the boat and threatened to break it to pieces.

The sailors were afraid. The boat was laden with goods to sell and now they threw these into the sea. Perhaps the lighter boat would ride the waves more easily.

All this while, Jonah was sleeping below deck.

The captain came to him. "Wake up, wake up," he shouted. "How can you sleep through this storm? You must pray to your God to save us all."

Jonah joined the other sailors and they drew lots to see who had provoked so great a storm. Jonah drew the shortest lot. "You have caused this rage," said the sailors. "But what have you done?"

"I am a Hebrew," Jonah replied. "And I worship the Lord, the maker of land and sea. And now I am running away from Him."

The sailors were terrified. "What must we do to calm the violent sea?"

"You must throw me overboard," said Jonah. "It is the only way to make the storm die down. It's my fault that you are in danger."

The sailors didn't want to kill Jonah. They tried all the harder to row back to land, but they could not. The storm grew even wilder than before.

Exhausted, the men cried out to God: "Oh Lord, please don't punish us for killing this innocent man. We are only doing as you wanted." And they took Jonah and threw him overboard.

Immediately, the sea became calm and the wind died away. The sailors were amazed by God's power. They made a sacrifice to Him and offered prayers of thanks.

And they took Jonah and threw him overboard.

Jonah sank deep beneath the waves. But God did not mean Jonah to die. He sent a great fish which swallowed the prophet whole. And so Jonah found himself sitting inside the belly of a fish.

For three day and three nights, Jonah lay in his strange, dark prison. And all the while he prayed to God.

"Lord, you have thrown me into the deep and out of your sight. Yet still I pray to you. The waters surrounded me, seaweed wrapped itself around my

head and I thought I was lost forever. But you have saved me. I remembered you, and I prayed to you. And now I thank you and I swear I will do as I have promised. Only the Lord can save."

And the Lord spoke to the fish and it threw up Jonah, out of its belly and on to dry land.

God spoke to Jonah again, telling him to go to Nineveh. And this time Jonah did as he was told.

Now Nineveh was a huge city - so large that it would take a man three days to walk around it. Jonah did not hesitate. He went straight into the heart of the city and called out the Lord's message. "Stop your evil and violent ways. If you do not, in forty days Nineveh will be completely destroyed," he warned.

So the people of Nineveh believed Jonah and God's word. Everyone, from the richest to the poorest, put on rough sackcloth, and began

Even the King of Nineveh took off his robes and dressed in sackcloth.

to fast - not a crumb of bread, not a drop of water passed their lips.

Even the king of Nineveh took off his golden robes and dressed in sackcloth. And he sat in ashes rather than on his magnificent throne.

The king and his people cried out to the Lord. "We will turn away from violence and our evil ways. Oh spare us, mighty God, from your fierce anger."

And God saw what they had done and heard their prayers. And He spared the city from destruction.

Jonah wasn't happy with God's decision. In fact, he was furious. He could not understand why God had shown such mercy to the people of Nineveh.

"Why have you been so kind?" he shouted at God. "This is why I didn't want to come to Nineveh - I knew you would change your mind, for you are too full of goodness.

"You should kill me now, Lord. I would rather be dead than alive!" he cried out in his fury.

The Lord only said, "Are you right to be angry?"

So Jonah went east out of the city.

He built a rough shelter and sat beneath it, and watched the city and waited. Would the Lord take any notice of his wishes?

The city slept peacefully. During the night, at God's command, an amazing vine grew up over Jonah's shelter. All through the day that followed, the vine shaded Jonah from the heat of the sun. The prophet was delighted.

The next day the vine was dead. God had sent a worm in the night and it had eaten the plant so that it withered away.

The day was extremely hot and windy. The sun beat down on Jonah's head and he felt faint with heat. Jonah's anger returned. "I am better off dead than alive!" he said again.

And God asked Jonah, "Are you right to be angry that the vine has died?"

"Yes, I am right to be angry," said Jonah. "The vine was a good thing."

And God explained his actions to Jonah.

"Why do you feel sorry about the vine dying? You didn't plant it and you did nothing to make it grow. It came in the night and died in the night.

"And yet the great city of Nineveh stands. Isn't it better that I should spare the lives of twelve thousand people than that of a single vine?"

 About this book 

All the stories in this book are retellings from the Bible, the collection of writings that are sacred, in different forms, to the Christian and Jewish religions. They are taken from various of the 39 books that make up the Hebrew Bible, Tanakh, or the Christian Old Testament.

Noah's Ark is taken from Genesis, the first book of the Bible. Genesis, which means beginning, is concerned with setting out the ancestory of the Hebrew peoples, amongst whom the Jewish religion began. Noah was the son of Lamech, who was a direct descendant of Adam, the first man. In turn, Noah's son Shem was a direct ancestor of Abraham, the first of the Patriachs (or founding fathers).

Jacob and Esau also comes from Genesis. It continues the story of the Hebrew family. Jacob was Abraham's grandson. He and his father Isaac were the other two Patriachs. God had given Abraham the fertile land of Canaan and now this land passed to Jacob. Later, God renamed Jacob Israel and his descendants become known as the Israelites. Jacob's sons and two of his grandsons gave their names to the twelve tribes of Israel.

Joseph and His Brothers retells the events which bring Genesis to a close. Joseph's story is partly a lead up to the great events of Exodus, the next book in the Bible, explaining how the Israelites came to Egypt from the land of Canaan. It also shows how God protected the Israelites, as His chosen people, saving them from famine just as before He had saved Noah and his family from the Flood.

Moses in the Bulrushes relates the events at the very beginning of Exodus: how Moses was chosen by God to lead the Israelites out of Egypt, where they had been enslaved. As He had once given Abraham the land of Canaan, God now promised the same land to Moses and the Israelites.

Exodus from Egypt tells how Moses fulfilled God's command and lead the Israelites out of Egypt (Exodus means 'the going out'). After the Israelites escaped from Egypt, they did not go straight to the promised land, they wandered through the wilderness for 40 years. Moses continued to lead them and, through him, God gave them the Ten Commandments. But Moses never reached the promised land, although he saw it from a distance. His great achievement was to bring the Israelites there, held together by strong laws and their faith in God.

David and Goliath comes from I Samuel, the ninth book in the Bible. The Israelites had established themselves in the lands of Canaan and formed a nation they called Israel. For about 250 years, Israel had been ruled by elders and priests, but Saul became its first king and David its second. Under David's rule, Israel became the most powerful country between the rivers Nile and Euphrates.

Daniel in the Lions' Den comes from Daniel, the twenty-seventh book of the Bible. In the 6th century BC, the Jewish kingdom of Judah (a region of Israel) came under the power of the Babylonian empire and many of its people were taken as slaves to serve in the empire's capital, Babylon. This period away from Israel became known as the Babylonian exile. The events in Daniel take place at this time but the book was probably written some 300 years later, when the Jewish people had returned to Israel but were once again under the control of a foreign power - this time the Greeks. The story of Daniel reminds people to keep their faith, even at times of great hardship.

The Story of Jonah retells the whole of Jonah, the thirty-second book of the Bible. It was probably written at about the same time as Daniel. Unlike the other stories in the collection, it is not concerned with the history of the Israelites and their Jewish descendants. It is a more personal story about Jonah's struggle to understand God and why He chooses to forgive the people of Nineveh.

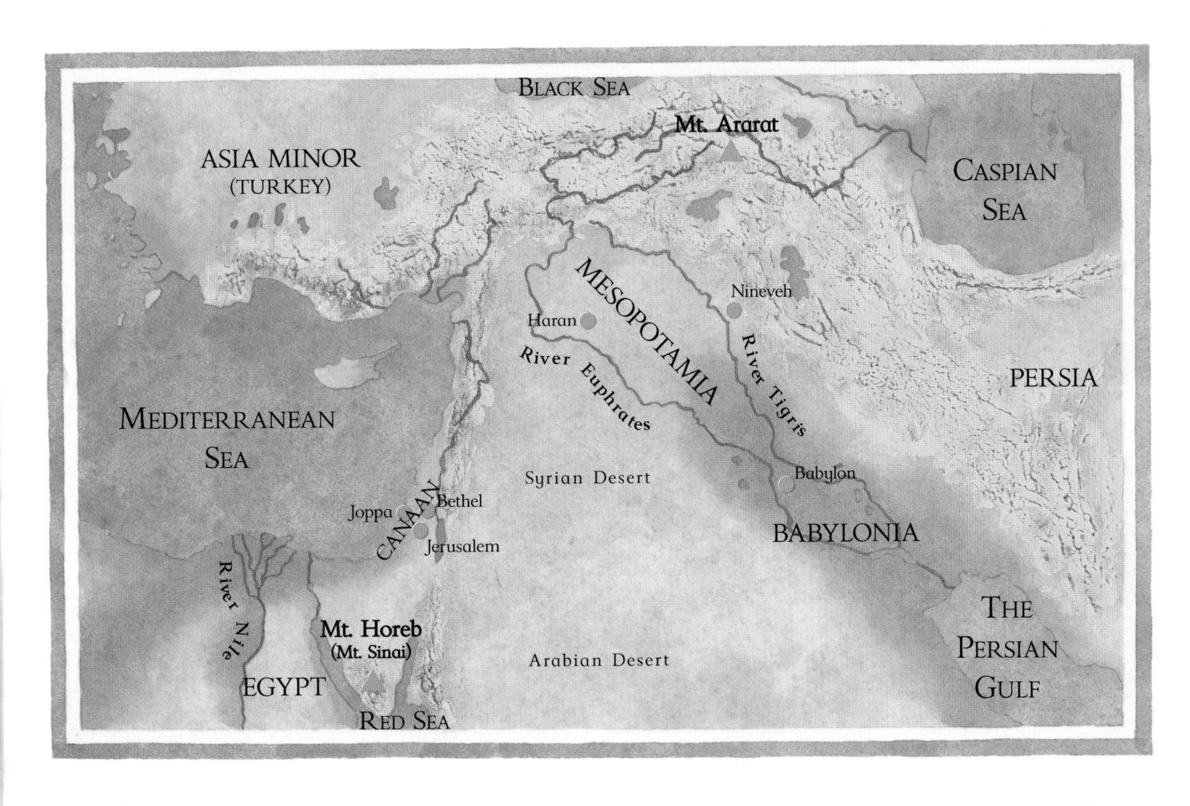

This map shows the area of the Middle East where the events in these stories took place.